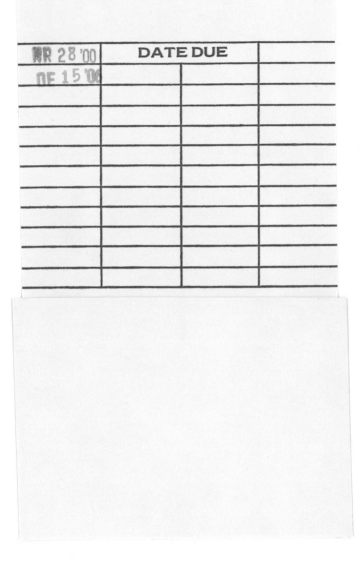

	DATE DUE		
MR 28 '00			
DE 15 '06			

SUPERSTARS OF FILM

brad pitt

Amy Dempsey

CHELSEA HOUSE PUBLISHERS
Philadelphia

First published in traditional hardback edition
© 1998 by Chelsea House Publishers.
Printed in Hong Kong
Copyright © Parragon Book Service Ltd 1995
Unit 13–17, Avonbridge Trading Estate, Atlantic Road
Avonmouth, Bristol, England BS11 9QD

Library of Congress Cataloging-in-Publication Data
Dempsey, Amy.
        Brad Pitt / by Amy Dempsey.
            p. cm. — (Superstars of film)
        Originally published : London : Parragon Books, 1996.
        Filmography: p.
        Includes index.
        Summary: Presents the life and career of the young Oscar-
nominated movie actor.
        ISBN 0-7910-4649-4 (hardcover)
        1. Pitt, Brad, 1963-   —Juvenile literature. 2. Actors—United
States—Biography—Juvenile literature. [1. Pitt, Brad, 1963-   .]
I.Title. II. Series.
PN2287.P54D46 1997
791.43'028'092—dc21
        [B]   97-26961
                                                                                                CIP
                                                                                                 AC

ACKNOWLEDGMENTS
Aquarius
Columbia (courtesy Kobal)
Geffen Pictures (courtesy Kobal)
MGM/Pathe (courtesy Kobal)
Mirror Syndication International
Morgan Creek/Davis Films (courtesy Kobal)
Paramount (courtesy Kobal)
Propaganda/Polygram/Viacom (courtesy Kobal)
Peter Sorel/New Line (courtesy Kobal)
Tr-Star/Bedford/Pangaea (courtesy Kobal)
Vega/Arena/Balthazar (courtesy Kobal)

CONTENTS

Brad Pitt

GROWING UP

On December 18, 1963, William Bradley Pitt was born in Shawnee, Oklahoma, to Bill and Jane Pitt. He was their first born, and to them the most beautiful baby in the world. Little could they have imagined that thirty-one years later the readers of *People* magazine would agree—voting their blue-eyed boy the "Sexiest Man Alive."

Shawnee was a small midwestern town (population 24,000) where Bill and Jane had grown up and where Bill worked as a manager for a trucking firm. When Bill received a better job offer in Springfield, Missouri, the young family made the move. Springfield was a much larger, growing town on the other side of the Ozark Mountains that served as the commercial center for the sprawling agricultural area of the surrounding plains. The family soon grew, with the birth of Douglas three years after Brad (as William had come to be called), and Julie two years later.

The Pitt children were raised in an atmosphere of love and respect where the importance of family and religion was stressed. They were taught to be polite and courteous and to live by the "golden rule"—do unto others as you would have others do unto you. The Pitt family regularly attended the South Haven Baptist Church, where Brad was a member of the choir. The church pianist recalls that even at this early age, it was impossible not to notice Brad. It was a warm, loving grounding for all the Pitt children and the family remains a close and caring one. The parents tried to instill in their children a sense of self-worth and confidence and encouraged them to try new things without fear of failure.

Bill Pitt's new job was demanding and required him to work long hours, so he was often away from home. Brad commented in *Vanity Fair,* "I understand that people work. My father spent thirty-six years, six days a week on the job." But when Bill was around, he made a concerted effort to spend quality time with his children, taking the family on trips to the nearby Ozark Mountains and to drive-in movies, and attending performances of their various activities. His straightforward, no-nonsense manner had a profound influence on Brad.

This happy family atmosphere paid off and by all accounts Brad was a popular, outgoing, sensitive child. He was a good student and an avid reader and he threw himself into a number of activities, giving each one his all. While at Kickapoo High School he participated in student government, the choir, school plays, and sports. The scar on his left cheekbone came from these days in the form of a missed fly ball in a baseball game. He also played on the school tennis team, and Brad recalls one incident when his father came to speak to him during the break in a match after Brad had been less than well behaved, throwing a temper tantrum on court. Instead of scolding Brad, Bill simply asked him if he was enjoying himself, to which Brad had to reply in the negative. His father then said, "Then don't do it"—words of wisdom that would stand Brad in good stead on a number of occasions.

From an early age Brad was popular with the girls. He recalls his first kiss, in fourth grade, when he met the girl in her garage, kissed her, and ran away. His first girlfriend was Kim Bell in junior high school. At thirteen, under the watchful eyes of his parents, Brad graduated to hosting kissing parties in the family basement, complete with beanbag

Relaxing in True Romance

chairs and flavored lip-gloss. His steady girlfriend in high school was Sara Hart, who went to a different school. They met at a high school debate and were immediately inseparable, spending all their free time together, going to each other's proms, and meeting each other's families.

By the time Brad was a teenager his main interests were films, art, and music. He remembers that the first film that really moved him was *Planet of the Apes* with Charlton Heston and Roddy McDowall; Elton John's song "Daniel" from the album *Captain Fantastic* inspired his interest in music. He began to take guitar lessons and dream of a career in music. Brad also enjoyed drawing and was quite good at it, carrying around a notebook to make sketches when the mood struck. Although he participated in school plays and musicals, his acting at that stage was simply another extracurricular activity.

When Brad got his driver's license—that momentous event symbolizing freedom and independence for the teenager—the family Buick was passed down to him and the world around him opened up. He began exploring, and falling in love with, the countryside around him. When he later achieved fame and financial success, he began to buy land in the mountains to use as a family retreat, acquiring six hundred acres where he could go to escape the chaos of Hollywood and be with his family.

As a well-rounded student with a good academic record, the question was not whether to go to college, but which one to attend. Brad chose the University of Missouri at Columbia, which has a reputable journalism school. He planned to major in journalism and then go into advertising with the aim of becoming an art director. Brad threw himself into university life, learning to work hard and play hard. He joined the Sigma Chi fraternity, moved into the frat house, and became involved in a social life revolving around *Animal House*-type pranks and parties.

By this time Brad was a six-foot tall, blond, blue-eyed

muscular hunk who was extremely popular with the girls. His relationship with Sara had ended with high school, so he was a now free man. Brad's growing popularity and desirability increased even more when he agreed to pose for the yearly campus calendar. His bare-chested photograph certainly made him a name around the campus, and the calendar sold out almost immediately. Little did he know that this was just the beginning of his career as a pinup.

For the most part, Brad thrived on college life. He successfully learned the lessons about growing up that are such an important part of the college experience—learning to live on his own without parental control, and being responsible for his own actions without having them around to bail him out. During his college days a serious car accident also brought about a real sense of his own mortality, something that many people don't think about until much later in life. As Brad explains, "I got hit by an eighteen-wheeler. Not much left of the car. Took the roof with it. Just turned into us and took us with him. No one was even hurt. It was just kind of like once we had a roof and now we don't." Fortunately Brad and his friends were in his very sturdy family Buick, which undoubtedly saved their lives. The car was replaced by a beaten-up Datsun that Brad named "Runaround Sue."

In Robert Redford's A River Runs Through It

HOLLYWOOD BECKONS

By the spring of 1986, his final semester in college, Brad was becoming increasingly confused about what to do with his life. Whether it was a result of the reality check of the car accident or a natural progression of events, he no longer felt able to take the expected route. The final term of college, particularly in mid-eighties, middle-class America, equaled interview suit, job, career, house, spouse, and family, but Brad needed to explore the world, question the expectations, find out who he was and what he really wanted to do. Once he realized that he had a choice and that there were other options to explore, he made his move. To the surprise of his friends and family, and probably himself, in May 1986, a month short of graduation, he packed up "Runaround Sue" and hit the road. Like so many before him, he decided to head west to seek his fortune. Telling his parents that he was going to the Art Center of the College of Design in Pasadena, he set off for Los Angeles to try to make it as an actor.

Brad arrived in Los Angeles with $325 to his name and no real idea about how to put his plan into action. He moved into a two-bedroom apartment in North Hollywood with seven other guys who were also trying to get started. They each had a corner of a room for their mattresses and belongings and shared the all-important answering machine, which was much more essential than furniture. Since he had no savings to allow him to be selective about where he worked, Brad embarked on a series of odd jobs to keep a roof over his head. The first was delivering refrigerators to college dorm rooms, followed by a stint as a telemarketer. When the telemarketing became too soul-destroying, he landed his next "character-building" job—as a chicken! El Pollo Loco, a fast-food chain of Mexican restaurants in southern California, can indeed claim that they once had Brad Pitt as their mascot, dressed up as a giant chicken to greet customers.

These jobs may have been less than fulfilling, but they did allow Brad to attend the rounds of open auditions. Although he found them frustrating, he met lots of people in the same boat and made many friends. He had brought his guitar with him and soon had plenty of people to jam with late into the night. Life in L.A. was an exciting challenge, and even though Brad had no formal acting training, he was convinced that he would make it if he persevered. While continuing the odd jobs, he got a part as an extra in *Less Than Zero*. Although it was nothing to write home about yet, it was a start; he was finally on screen, albeit briefly, and he got his first paycheck from his newly chosen field. Brad was heartened by his success and decided to give himself at least a year to try to get a real part before having to rethink his life plan.

Brad knew that he needed both an acting coach and an agent. But acting lessons cost money, and although agents can help land roles, they generally require their clients to have previous experience before taking them on. His new job, however, would lead him to both. Brad was now working as a driver for a strip-a-gram company. It was better paid than his previous jobs and the hours were at night, leaving his days free for auditions. The girls that he drove around were for the most part like himself, aspiring actors doing whatever it took to get by while they pursued their dream. One of the girls offered to introduce Brad to her coach, Roy

London, a well-respected acting coach who had had a number of success stories, including Michelle Pfeiffer and Sharon Stone. London agreed to take him on and Brad threw himself into the lessons, working hard to learn his craft. As a result of these classes came the meeting that would ultimately lead to his big break.

A woman in one of his acting classes had an audition with an agent. She asked Brad to go along and read the male role for her. Brad was happy to oblige, knowing that the only way to learn more about the business was to seize every opportunity that came his way. In typical Hollywood fashion the agent wanted to sign Brad and not the woman auditioning. The agent recognized that Brad had "it," that extra something that no amount of lessons can teach, a certain charisma that makes an impression on the audience. Brad was soon to be on his way.

Within a month of signing, Brad auditioned for *Dallas* and got a part. It was a small part—as the boyfriend of Shalane McCall, who played the role of Priscilla Presley's daughter in the series—but it was a real part nonetheless. Brad called his parents to tell them the news and to confess that he hadn't been going to art school at all, to which his father replied, "Yeah, I thought so."

In *US* magazine Brad recalled his first day on the set. "It was exciting-scary. That thrill. If I remember correctly, they kinda left me on my own. Like 'OK, do your job. . . .' And I was like, 'But-but-but, Wait a sec. I just got here from Missouri, see? You don't understand.'" Although he only had a small part, he was included in several episodes, which meant that both fans and people in the business saw his face and took note. He had his first mention in teen magazines, about his alleged off-set romance with his on-set partner, and his first taste of what it was like to have his life monitored and exaggerated by the media. According to the *National Enquirer* his relationship with Shalane lasted six weeks, and "when Brad stopped dating her, she was devastated and cried for three days, telling friends, 'I loved Brad more than anything in the world!'" While the hounding would become more intense and invasive as his career blossomed, keeping his name in the press and building his fan base at this early stage could do nothing but good.

The stint on *Dallas* was followed by a week on the daytime soap opera *Another World,* and then his agent began sending him out on auditions for sitcoms. Again the parts were small, but it was work, and good experience. He had parts in *Growing Pains* and then *Head of the Class,* where he met Robin Givens. Givens had just recently split up with Mike Tyson and she and Brad began seeing each other. Their relationship lasted about six months, ending shortly after a jealous Tyson visited Givens when Brad was at her house. Fortunately the meeting was not violent.

Parts followed in the TV shows *21 Jump Street* and *thirtysomething.* Edward Zwick and Marshall Herskovitz, the directors of *thirtysomething,* commented at the time, "He caused such a stir on the set. He was so good-looking and so charismatic and such a sweet guy, everybody knew he was going places." How right they were.

While the work continued to come in fairly constantly and Brad was able to survive financially from acting, he had yet to get anything more than a guest spot or a minor role. He continued to apply himself to acting classes and was determined that he would progress beyond being a TV hunk. In 1989 he auditioned for and got his first real part in a film, *Cutting Class,* a low-budget teenage slasher film in the *Friday the 13th* genre aimed primarily at the video and drive-in market. Although the film was "awful," as Brad later called it, he was on his way in a new medium. While filming, he met Jill Schoelen, who was playing one of the leads, and they became an item for a while.

Next followed a part in a television movie, *The Image,* which led to another project, starring in an episode of *Tales from the Crypt,* called "King of the Road." Brad played a tattooed, leather-jacketed street thug who kidnaps the local policeman's daughter to force him to drag race for her. Although it was a late-night cable project with a weak, derivative script, it helped to prove that Brad could carry more weight than bit parts required. He got a part in another straight-to-video movie, *Happy Together,* in which he again played a teenager. While aware how fortunate he was to have made it so far in the three years he had been in Hollywood, Brad wanted to move on to more substantial roles and more mature characters. At almost twenty-six, he was beginning to get frustrated with playing high school and college students—he wanted to play a man, not a boy. His next venture would unexpectedly help with this image change—his appearance in a Levi's commercial.

Brad as JD in Thelma and Louise

THE NEW HEARTTHROB

The Levi's commercial was Brad's first foray into television advertising, and he was chosen for his looks. Although not a challenging career move, doing television advertising—particularly for a product like Levi's—is quick, easy money that provides lots of exposure. The commercial was for the European market, and Brad's rugged, "all-American" look was what they wanted. The ad's soundtrack featured The Clash's song "Should I Stay or Should I Go?" and as a result of the commercial the song returned to the charts (after ten years off) and benefited from revitalized sales. The commercial also showed off Brad's physique and handsome face to their full advantage, and helped to establish him as a sex symbol.

In 1990 the work continued to pour in. He was cast as one of the leads in *Glory Days,* a Fox-TV series about four male friends and how they progress after high school. Six episodes were made and aired, but the series did not catch on and it was dropped. Although disappointed, Brad did not have time to become too disheartened, for shortly afterward he was offered two large parts—one in a film and one in a TV movie.

Although *Across the Tracks* was a B-movie, the part Brad was offered was larger than any he had played so far and he was to receive second billing. Top billing went to Rick

17

Schroder, who was well known from his days as a child actor in *The Champ* and from the television series *Silver Spoons*. It was a story about two brothers, the bad (Schroder) and the good (Pitt), and the tensions and competitions of their relationship. Brad's character was a track star, and he threw himself into training for the role. Though it was a low-budget, small film, Brad's part had just as much weight as Schroder's and it was his big chance to prove that he could portray a full character. The film received a very limited release and very little critical attention, but for Brad it was a major accomplishment; he had carried a leading role as a "real" actor, not just as a pretty face.

The made-for-TV movie that Brad worked on next, *Too Young to Die?*, was important for him both professionally and socially. Based on the true story of the first minor to be sentenced to death, it raised the question of whether teens should be tried as adults and given the death penalty. Brad played a despicable low-life who used, abused, and goaded the teen, played by Juliette Lewis, into murdering her former lover. It was Brad's meatiest role to date and one that provided many challenges. First, he had to play against his primary asset, his looks, by making himself look as slimy and unappealing as possible. He also had to portray convincingly the evil of the character as well as the hold he had over the girl. His winning smile turned into a leer, and the charisma that he exuded playing more sympathetic characters worked just as well to hold the audience's attention when playing a repulsive one. It was Juliette Lewis's first starring role and both she and Brad turned in strong performances. This was to be Brad's last television movie, as he was now better equipped to tackle the big screen.

Brad and Juliette worked well together, researching their characters, listening to music, and generally getting to know each other. The chemistry between the two certainly came through in their performances. Brad assumed it was the result of working together in an intense situation and kept their relationship platonic while making the film. Once the film finished, however, both Brad and Juliette realized that they wanted to spend more time together. They were soon inseparable and were seen everywhere together. The age difference (Juliette was only sixteen—ten years younger than Brad) didn't prove to be much of a problem, for Juliette acted much older than her real age. She had been working steadily in television since the age of twelve and had been legally emancipated from her parents since the age of fourteen. Since then she had been living in Hollywood, first with a family friend, the actress Karen Black, and then in an apartment with Trish Merkens, her best friend. Working and supporting herself for a few years had taught her to be much more independent and mature than many others of her age.

As their relationship progressed they moved in together to a bungalow in Beechwood Canyon. They provided support for each other and created a safe haven to return to when the pressures of work became too much. Both Brad and Juliette were intensely committed to their careers, which were both to shift gears dramatically in the forthcoming year: 1991 was the year of *Cape Fear* for Juliette and of *Thelma & Louise* for Brad.

When William Baldwin backed out of Ridley Scott's new film, *Thelma & Louise,* to accept a larger part in *Backdraft,* Brad got the call that would change his life and make him a household name. He went to read with Geena Davis and got the part of JD, the small-time thief who teaches Thelma (Davis) how to rob. *Thelma & Louise,* starring Davis and Susan Sarandon, was one of the most controversial and talked about films of 1991. It sparked debate both in the media and on the streets; the press coverage and word-of-mouth publicity was phenomenal. Brad could not have dreamed of a better vehicle for his major film debut. He was working with big names—Davis, Sarandon, and Harvey Keitel—in a role that he could really make his own, that of the southern charmer: polite, good-looking, seductive, and a rogue. Although only a small part, it included one of the most-talked about love scenes in a long time. One review described it as one of the rare love scenes that manages to be "funny and truly erotic at the same time." The scene was anything but sensuous to shoot; one technician recalls that Brad was "absolutely charming, very shy and nervous," and that his biggest concern was what his mother would think. The scene made Brad into an instant heartthrob. Rumors of an affair with Davis, who had recently split up with her husband, Jeff Goldblum, while filming, only served to heighten his image as an irresistible hunk.

Brad was pleased with his performance, but had no idea of the impact until the premiere of the film. As Juliette recalls, "I went to Brad's premiere for *Thelma & Louise.* Everyone was screaming, 'Brad! Brad! Over here!' The flash-bulbs are exploding in your face. It's like a brainwashing trip. You could be brainwashed into being forever dispersed and just lost!" Fortunately, although overwhelmed and flattered, Brad did not succumb to the adulation, realizing that this attention would pass as soon as the next new star appeared. It had happened thousands of times before and would again, and the challenge for Brad was how to capitalize on his newfound fame without being forever typecast as a hunk. His instincts proved correct when a few months later he and Juliette were at the premiere of *Cape Fear,* her big launch. As the cameras turned on him, he was asked how he liked being on *Beverly Hills 90210,* to which he just laughed and told them it wasn't him, and they were gone. "I mean, just like that. Fade to black. I got a kick out of that."

Brad and Juliette were now Hollywood's golden couple. Young, attractive, and successful, they were wined, dined, and pursued for numerous new projects. The scripts kept coming in and Brad chose three that he thought would bring challenges, different both from one another and from *Thelma & Louise.* The first was *The Favor,* a comedy of errors with Elizabeth McGovern, in which Brad hoped to show his

Pitt meets Davis in Thelma and Louise

comic potential. Unfortunately the end result was forgettable and the film remained unreleased until 1994, when it went straight to video to capitalize on Brad's growing fame. The cast, particularly McGovern and Pitt, stood out for making solid characters from stereotyped clichés, but it wasn't enough to ensure the success of the film. According to *People* magazine, "*The Favor* cannot lay claim to a single plot twist that is at all new or interestingly redone. . . . The cast members, particularly Pullman and Pitt, deserve an audience's deepest, deepest sympathy."

Brad's next project was a starring role, albeit in a low-budget art film that was expected to garner only a cult audience. The film was Tom DiCillo's *Johnny Suede,* about a would-be rock idol. The role required a portrayal with subtlety, sincerity, and innocence to keep the character from seeming a total simpleton and completely laughable. Brad pulled this off admirably, using the small gestures and facial expressions that were proving so effective in his acting. *Johnny Suede* did well critically and at film festivals, even winning the Golden Leopard award for Best Film at Locarno, Switzerland. But the praise for Brad's performance, DiCillo's directing, and the film as a whole was not enough to make it a box-office success, and its quirky nature bypassed most audiences. After a short time in mainstream cinemas, it moved to the arthouse circuit and then to video. Brad was disappointed because he liked the film, although he had known from the start that this was a film more about his development as an actor than his career advancement. He enjoyed working on the film and hanging out with the cast and crew, something he would continue to do even as his fame grew. He continues to work on a film as a member of a team in which everyone's role is considered vital, a positive attitude that has been commented upon by many who have worked with him.

The would-be rock star, Johnny Suede

Brad with 'toon seductress in Ralph Bakshi's Cool World

TESTING TIMES

By the time *Johnny Suede* was making its brief appearance, Brad was already in the midst of another project—*Cool World* by Ralph Bakshi, a well-known animator whose new project was to go far beyond *Who Framed Roger Rabbit?* Parts in the film were highly sought after—more than two hundred actors auditioned for the part of the humanoid policeman, Frank Harris. Bakshi wanted Brad and had to convince the producers that he was the one for the role. Gabriel Byrne, Kim Basinger, and Brad were cast. This type of acting was a whole new experience because most of the scenes required "interaction" with animated cartoons that would be drawn in later. Standing on a soundstage surrounded by technicians and acting to the air was both humbling and difficult. The final result was just too much, since the human actors were overwhelmed by the animation. Perhaps *Variety*'s review best captured the problem: "Bakshi has let his imagination run wild with almost brutal vigor, resulting in a guerrilla-like sensual assault unchecked by any traditional rules of storytelling." It was a resounding flop.

While Brad had been busy doing three films in a row, Juliette had been busy working on Woody Allen's *Husbands and Wives,* and the time apart was hard for both of them. Whenever their schedules allowed they would hang out at home, dodging the media and catching up on their relationship. They put the same effort into that as they did their work, and it remained surprisingly strong through all the enforced separations. They were confident of their feelings for each other and that helped them through the times apart. Juliette said about Brad, "He's the most naturally monogamous creature I've ever run into, male or female."

Brad's three films since *Thelma & Louise* had not been box-office successes, but were important in showing the wider range of characters Brad was capable of playing. While his looks were certainly still a prime asset, his skills as an actor were rapidly developing. Brad knew he had more to offer than just a pretty face and a good body and was constantly on the lookout for scripts that would offer him the chance to prove it. When Robert Redford asked him to read for a part in the new film he was directing, *A River Runs Through It,* Brad was thrilled. Redford's participation implied quality, dedication, and certain exposure and the character was unlike any other that Brad had played. It was a story of two brothers growing up in Montana in the early part of the century and Brad was to play Paul, the golden boy going downhill fast.

Preparation for the film included learning fly-fishing, no mean feat in Los Angeles. He practiced casting from the rooftops of buildings in Hollywood, catching himself in the back of the head a number of times before getting the hang of it. When they set up in Montana, fishing lessons continued, as did coaching in the regional accent. Brad spent his free time meeting the locals and exploring the beautiful countryside. Craig Sheffer played older brother Norman, with Redford doing the voice-overs of Norman as an older man reminiscing. Several reviews, not unkindly, noted Brad's uncanny resemblance to the young Robert Redford. The *New York Times* remarked, "The resemblance probably has less to do with the director's ego than with Mr. Pitt's charismatic presence and ability to project Paul's glamorous aura so powerfully." Another critic wrote, "In Paul's tones of

Casting a line in A River Runs Through It

voice, and the expression of his eyes, often seen in close-up, can be read, like reflections on shifting water, the tiniest fleeting presences of jealousy giving way to generosity over Norman's good fortune . . . until, for one shattering instant outside the gambling hall, Paul's eyes give away the desperation that will destroy him." Under Redford's direction, Brad convincingly became Paul and the film was a popular success. Brad himself did not think it was his best work but agreed that the film was beautifully handled by Redford.

By now most critics were willing to concede that Brad had charisma, that the camera loved him, and that he was star material. But Brad was not about to believe the hype, for he still had to prove to the critics and to himself that he was a professional, serious actor with staying power. He continually seeks roles that will stretch his limits, to see just how far he can go—to be the best actor that he can be. "I asked for it, I picked the hardest ones I could find. And, damned right, they were," Brad said later. His next role, as a sociopathic hillbilly serial killer in *Kalifornia,* proved this. The character of Early Grayce was as far away from golden boy Paul as possible. The other attraction was that Juliette was also cast and they were both excited about working together again. In preparation for the role Brad put on twenty pounds and let his hair and beard grow long and greasy. "I wanted to do one of those trailer-dwelling, greasy nail guys. . . . It's the farthest thing from Golden Boy." Brad's supporting actors were David Duchonvy (now of *The X-Files*) and Michele Forbes as the yuppie-couple contrast to Brad and Juliette's lower-class characters. Despite the draw of its stars and heavy advertising the film did not do well at the box office; it was apparently too dark and unglamorous for most audiences. Brad's performance as the ugly, evil, menacing Early was, however, noticed by a few critics. "Mr. Pitt lends nasty credence to Early's viciousness," said the *New York Times,* continuing, "*Kalifornia* confirms that Mr. Pitt is an interesting, persuasive actor."

*Craig Sheffer and the young Redford look-alike
in* A River Runs Through It

After the dark intensity of *Kalifornia,* Brad craved some fun, which came in the form of Floyd, the dopey pothead in the Quentin Tarantino–scripted *True Romance.* His small part provided a little light relief, and again he played it to perfection. After the few days of filming it was time to take a break and concentrate on domestic issues, primarily his relationship with Juliette. After three years, Juliette wanted to get married, but Brad was not yet ready for that step. After a lot of talk and tears the two decided to go their separate ways. Brad rented a house and moved out. It was a hard time for both of them and Brad filled the empty evenings by going to bars or staying in, listening to music and watching hours of mindless late-night television. The days were long: after such a long stint of constant work he was unused to free time between projects and he and his agent had yet to find a suitable script for his next move.

His life started to look up when he met actress Jitka Pohlodek at a party. She was pretty and exotic, had two bobcats as pets, and supposedly came from Czechoslovakia. They began seeing each other and life seemed less empty. Then came not one but two scripts from his agent. The first one he read was *Legends of the Fall,* to be directed by Edward Zwick and produced by Marshall Herskovitz, long-time collaborators from the days of *thirtysomething.* Brad jumped on it. As he told *Premiere,* "This story was one of the only ones where I've ever said, 'I'm the guy for this one.' I've always felt there was someone else who could do a little better. But not on this one: this story I felt like I knew from the beginning to the end. I knew the stops and I knew the turns. This one meant more." Brad was so committed to getting the film made and being in it that he lowered his salary and became production partners with Zwick, both of them deferring large parts of their salaries. Zwick then signed Sir Anthony Hopkins, who was "in the mood to do a Western" and by December 1992 TriStar was also in, committing $30 million to the production.

Juliette and Brad together in Kalifornia

Hollywood love scenes, Brad giggled and replied, "It's not the most romantic setting, you know?" Especially if, like Brad, you are worrying about what your mother will think. "My poor mom! . . . So you throw a little music on, and try to forget about all the people staring at you. I got that, actually, from Ridley [Scott], because he let us play music during that Geena Davis scene."

Straight from the *Legends* shoot Brad joined the set of *Interview with the Vampire,* which was mired in its own problems. Anne Rice vociferously criticized various aspects of the film, from rewrites to the casting of Tom Cruise as Lestat. When she heard that Pitt had also been cast, she said disgustedly, "It's like casting Huck Finn and Tom Sawyer." River Phoenix had just died of an overdose and his part had to be recast. Tom Cruise and Brad had very different working styles that led to rumors of conflicts, which both repeatedly denied. Whatever the case, the film was made and Brad was relieved when it was finished. "I hated doing this movie. Hated it! My character is depressed from the beginning to the end. Five and a half months of that is too much."

It had been an exhausting year, and Brad now turned his attention to setting up house and getting his life in order. He decided that the relationship with Jitka wasn't meant to be and that it was time to move on. He began house hunting to find somewhere he could really call home. When he saw the house that had once been owned by horror-show hostess Elvira, he knew he had found the right place. It was set in several acres with a pool, a pond, and a cave and plenty of trees to shield it from the public—it was perfect. He moved in, along with the forty chameleons from his time with Jitka. Now that Brad had the space, he got three large dogs—Purty, Todd Potter, and Saudi—and he was content. He also spent time with his family in the six hundred acres he had acquired in the Ozarks, before chaos set in again.

Tom Cruise and Brad in Interview with the Vampire

Henry Thomas, Brad, and Aidan Quinn in Legends of the Fall

GOLDEN BOY

If anyone was unaware of Brad's existence before, by the end of 1994 everyone had heard of him. *Interview with the Vampire* opened in August, the same month he was featured in a cover story in *Rolling Stone*. The *Rolling Stone* issue sold out and the film brought in $38.7 million on its first weekend. A few weeks later, the *Vanity Fair* issue with Brad on the cover also flew off the newsstands.

Interview got lots of extra publicity, ranging from Oprah Winfrey walking out saying that it was too violent, to Anne Rice taking out a two-page print ad to praise Cruise as Lestat and to apologize for her earlier remarks. She also praised Brad in the *Vampire Chronicle* fan magazine: "The Barbie Doll from Hell [her nickname for Brad] was a hell of a Louis in *Interview,* upturned nose and all . . . he was beautiful as Louis, how fortunate we were." The film critics, however, were not so kind, almost universally panning the film and the acting. But their opinions did not seem to matter at all, and fans of Rice, Cruise, and Pitt continued to flock to the film, bringing in $105 million in three months. Brad's portrayal of Louis as the beautiful, romantic, tortured soul had women of all ages swooning and they wanted more.

They didn't have to wait long, because *Legends of the Fall* was in theaters by Christmas. The film grossed $60 million in its first two months and Brad's stardom was guaranteed.

In his role as Tristan, the romantic, tragic hero, Brad won the crowds' hearts. His magnetism and charisma brought the part alive. Aidan Quinn said of his performance, "I happened onto some dailies that were on tape, and saw him at the grave, and he was just devastating. Brad's got a very traditional, manly kind of persona, so to see that man fighting the emotion and not winning—there was stuff he was adding that wasn't scripted—was just so powerful, watching it spill out."

The reviews for the film and for Brad were mixed, but again it didn't matter to his fans. The film was nominated for two Golden Globe awards, one for Brad's acting, although it did not win either. *Rolling Stone* declared, "Pitt carries the picture. The blue-eyed boy who seemed a bit lost in *Interview with the Vampire* proves himself a bona fide movie star, stealing every scene he's in." *People* magazine observed, "Sometimes his portrayal of a man at war with himself is moving; at other times, he seems to be all attitude." Most critics thought the film as a whole overblown and too glossy, without enough substance. When Brad saw the final cut he was tempted to agree: "By taking out as much as they did, the movie becomes too mushy. If I'd known where it was going to end up, I'd have fought against the cheese. . . . This is a good movie. There are just moments where, if it was reduced to that, if that's all we were going to see of him, I would have whittled it down. I wouldn't have shown so much."

In the midst of the run of *Legends of the Fall,* in January 1995, *People* magazine named Brad "Sexiest Man Alive," further underlining his status as heartthrob of the nation and sending yet more people to see the film. His popularity continued to grow and Brad had to adjust to a new lifestyle where everyone wanted him. He could no longer enjoy his old pastimes, such as going to bars and listening to bands. With his face plastered all over the television, billboards, and magazines, the only options open to him were to stay at

Enjoying a picnic in Legends of the Fall

Brad as Detective Mills in Seven

home or go to celebrity hideaways such as the Viper Room, owned by Johnny Depp, or the House of Blues, also frequented by Michael Stipe.

Brad had never been one for the Hollywood scene and now that he had time to hang out with other actors of his age, he was not impressed. "I met a bunch of people, and it was that whole competitive, look-over, high-school-cafeteria thing. It was a shame. What's with that?" He was also not interested in the drug scene that accompanied so much of it, telling *Movieline,* "I've seen a lot of young actors go through that. They think they'll lose their creativity going straight. So many people—I even had the notion that you had to be miserable to be great. But then you gotta say, well, why does everyone either die from drugs, or quit? So how good can it be? Very simple question. Very tough answer. I don't trust drugs."

By the time of the *People* magazine tag, Brad was already at work on two more projects, *Seven* and *Twelve Monkeys.* Again it meant tight shooting schedules—Brad was only available for fifty-five days to film *Seven* before moving on. He was very enthusiastic about being a part of the film and had to convince the director, David Fincher, that he knew what he was letting himself in for. As Fincher explained in *Empire,* "I told him, 'This is not a major thing. This is a minor movie for everybody involved—and that's how we've got to keep looking at it. It's a little, tiny movie and it's just an experiment to let everybody do what they do and everybody invest in these people, and hopefully we can trick an audience into loving them or being fascinated by them, but it is going to be a gritty, little, hand-held . . . scrungy cop movie.'"

Although it was a dark, psychological thriller about a serial killer committing murders based on the seven deadly sins, Brad found playing the naive Detective Mills a welcome light relief after the depressing Louis in *Interview.* He also enjoyed doing physical, outdoor work again, although that too had its downside when he put his arm through a car window. As Brad told *US* magazine, "I was trying the do-your-own stunt thing. You know, that Joe Mannix approach? And I bit it. Hard. Basically, it was a matter of me trying to be cool and failing miserably. I slipped and went right through a car window. I wore a cast for the rest of the film. I did a lot of "pocket" acting. My first thought, being the sick, twisted actor guy that I am, was like: Oh, cool. I hope they got that!" They didn't. But *Seven* (which also starred Morgan Freeman and Gwyneth Paltrow), turned out to be anything but a minor movie. It was both a popular and a critical hit; even the critics finally conceded that Brad was an accomplished actor and not just a pretty face.

Next was Terry Gilliam's futuristic thriller *Twelve Monkeys,* in which Brad plays a mental patient. Again Brad lobbied for the part. "It was something that I normally wouldn't have been chosen for. And I understand that. People don't know what you're capable of until you prove it. So I met with him [Gilliam] several times to try to get him to take a chance on me. And he did. And that was very cool of him, because he isn't into the name game. It's like, 'I don't care who you are, cheesy movie guy.' He wants what's best. So he took a chance with me, and I appreciate that."

It was a chance well taken, as Brad's frenzied performance earned him an Academy Award nomination for Best Supporting Actor (although he lost out to Kevin Spacey for his role in *The Usual Suspects*). Gilliam attributes Brad's motivation to, among other things, the recent *People* magazine vote. "He found that appalling and was running as far away as possible. It was like they were dismissing him as a male bimbo, as just a bit of beefcake. And it made him so determined to never be accused of that again. With the validation of the Oscar [nomination] Brad can finally feel that he will be taken seriously."

By this time Brad was going out with Gwyneth Paltrow, who played his wife in *Seven*. They had met early in 1994 but did not become an item until they met again in

Morgan Freeman, Brad, and Gwyneth Paltrow in Seven

preproduction. When not working, the couple divided their time between his L.A. home and her New York apartment. As a successful actress dating the "world's sexiest man," she found the hardest thing to be the constant press intrusion. While the couple accepted most of it as part of being a celebrity, one incident went too far. In April of 1995 the couple went on a much-needed vacation to the Caribbean island of St. Bart's, where they were caught on camera and nude pictures were printed all over the world. Brad told the story to Margy Rochlin in *US* magazine, "Well, there are some magical poses! We were sort of operating under the Adam and Eve philosophy. And we'd just go about our day . . . and . . . there I am, in this . . . pose. It was enough to make me want to bury my head in the sand." After that the couple had to be constantly on their guard, but Brad was pretty philosophical about the incident, saying in the same interview, "But who really cares? I have one of the greatest jobs in the world, we see the country, our families are taken care of, what? I mean, there's a trade-off. . . . So be it." Though the couple seemed very much in love, after a seven month engagement Brad and Gwynneth decided to end their relationship.

In Brad's continual quest to do new and challenging roles that he finds interesting and that confound his sex-symbol image, he appeared in Jean-Jacques Annaud's *Seven Years in Tibet* (which involved sleeping in a tent in the Himalayas for five months while shooting) and *Devil's Own,* in which Brad played an IRA man to Harrison Ford's New York cop. As one of Hollywood's most sought-after actors, his asking price keeps escalating. He was reputed to command $8 million for *Seven Years in Tibet*—a far cry from $7 an hour as the El Pollo Loco chicken ten years earlier. Brad has thought about this issue as well: "It gets so crazy out there, people have no concept of money and the figures they offer can be crazy. I don't really know how I feel about it. Bottom line, are actors worth it? No, they're not. But if someone offers it to you are you going to say no? I know I'm not . . .There should always be a balance in salaries, they go up, they go down, but to me the important thing is the characters you're offered."

By all accounts Brad is a polite, charming, down-to-earth man with a good head on his shoulders. He has followed his own path and instincts to success and has avoided falling prey to all the hype surrounding him. He has finally proven to the Hollywood community what he has always believed: that he is a talented, multifaceted actor with much more to offer than just his good looks. Brad has shown that he is a force to be reckoned with and that he is here to stay.

FILMOGRAPHY

The year refers to the first release date of the film.

1989   *Cutting Class*
1989   *Happy Together*
1991   *Across the Tracks*
1991   *Thelma & Louise*
1991   *Johnny Suede*
1992   *Cool World*
1992   *A River Runs Through It*
1993   *Kalifornia*
1993   *True Romance*
1994   *The Favor*
1994   *Interview with the Vampire*
1994   *Legends of the Fall*
1995   *Seven*
1996   *Twelve Monkeys*
1996   *Sleepers*
1996   *Seven Years in Tibet*
1997   *Devil's Own*
1997   *Meet Joe Black*

INDEX

INDEX